From One Curious Kid to Another

Erica Lundy

BookLeaf Publishing

Presentation by *BookLeaf Publishing*

Web: www.bookleafpub.com

E-mail: info@bookleafpub.com

ISBN: 9789357211437

First edition 2022

DEDICATION

To Scott who sees the child in me and is always willing to play.

ACKNOWLEDGEMENT

"When working with kids, growth is inevitable. Usually it's yours."
To my students everywhere, who have taught me so much.

PREFACE

This collection of eclectic thoughts contains my hopes and dreams for our future generations. In this unpredictable and challenging world, the ground we balance our toes on is everchanging. Being kind and curious is the only way to grow.

Breath. Really.

Take a deep breath.
Really.
Don't just do it to get it over with.
Fill up your belly like a balloon.

In- like your smelling a fresh baked
chocolate chip cookie.
Out- like the soup
is too hot.

Ten times.
A hundred times.
A million times.
A life of times.

Until you aren't scared anymore.
Until you aren't mad.

Until the only sound you hear
Is the soft, specific sound
of your own inhale and exhale
in stillness.

Did You See that Bug?

Did you see that bug?
No. That one there.

I saw your eyes hesitate and take a step back.
Isn't it easier to walk away?

Instead,
Step closer.

Do you see its spots?
It's waggling antenna
Its millions of legs?
The better to walk with my dear.

Gaze through the icy glaze of its wings.

If you're still,
It may fly to your shoulder.
Can you pick it up?

It ticklishly tangles though your fingers.

Lift the log
Leave the squeals for the swing set.
Look.

Two Too Many Birthdays

I'm waiting.

False start. With a penalty.

Hoping won't work.
It isn't best to get your hopes up.

Wishing is no good either.
Two too many birthdays wishing on candles
without the perfect present.

I see you everywhere
In the 29 daily smiles.

What will your smile look like?
How hard will you laugh?

I see you everywhere.
Where are you hiding?
Are you ready yet?
Are we there yet?

We will celebrate together. Two-gether.
Three-gether.

Sharing our smiles
Laughing all the way home.

Time for a Bike Change

Time for a bike change

Sometimes, you need the slick handling of a
road bike.
For the winding mountain roads
for fast descents and uphill climbs

Hours of suffering for a sprint finish.
Only to lose at the line.

So it's time for a bike change.

And sometimes you get the big air
they take away the ramp and pull the bottom
from under you
The mountains enormous.
Insurmountable.

Don't writhe on the floor.
The job isn't done.
The race not won.

Roll over the rough stuff
Put air back in the tires.
Time for a bike change.

Sometimes the course is disaster
Your shoes stick in the messy mud.
A pass on the inside, with the most heart
Only to drop a chain

Time for a bike change.

Life is like riding a bicycle
to keep your balance
you must
keep

changing your bike.

If You Ever Go Camping

If you ever go camping,
and I hope you do,
don't put your shoes close enough to the fireside
to
melt.

But, melt the chocolate so it runs down your
chin.
A flaming ball of sugar stuck between two sweet
crisps.

Ignore the shadows behind,
for the darkness is deafening out there.
Focus on the flames in front

An excellent time to get to listen
to the real you.

Find the perfect stick, or rock, or moment to
remember.

Chart it with the gasping points of light
sprinkled in the
be-speckled sky.

Can you name them?
I know a few.
I am happy to share as we sit craning our necks
to see one swiftly shoot by.

Those waiting moments
Hushed and still
before the streak of light
makes it all worth waiting for.

If you ever go camping,
Listen for the birds.
A red hooded warbler, or pink toed grouse.
Or other such nonsense to make you,
a city dweller feel out of your depths.

But dive in deep,
to the buzz of the fly floating beside you.
Following you
and your big footsteps

from the wild back to camp.

Bring back with you
the wind in the trees
It feels stronger there.
The smell of the earth
It feels deeper there

and the warmth and cozy
of the sky resting on your shoulders.

If you ever go camping,
as you drive back into town
back along the city roads
keep close

the call of the wild.

Mildly Destructive Science

Mildly destructive science.
The best kind.
The kind that makes the table sticky, and maybe gets something
on the ceiling.

I won't be mad.
For in the name of science,
I can't be.

Dissect, deconstruct, decompose
denature, dissolve, describe

Discover

Make a mess
to help you make sense of it all.

I'll help. I promise.

We'll build that catapult
or is it
a
trebuchet

We'll fling to learn physics

Stir the chemical cauldron to
compose notes of chemistry

We might get some on the carpet.

We'll tromp through the trails of the
open space casting tracks.
Dripping the plaster a little bit in the dirt.
Believing in the blessings of biology

Mildly destructive science.
Like magic but real.

Costco

One day we will take a trip
to
Costco

Its big wide aisles and
high
ceilings
will make you feel small

But the movement of
people will sweep
you from row to row

From the front seat
of a metal cart

you will kick your legs
Let's go!

There is a thing over there!

Words not yet ready to name
but eyes ready to see.

There is another thing

over there.
And there.

Cookies by the pound
Sheet cakes to sleep in.

Clothes to touch
and smells to smell.

Chips by the gallon
stuck in between surfboards and strawberries

Don't worry.
We'll do the full tour.
We usually do.

Our date night stroll
to Costco
has a new recruit

See the soft rugs standing at
attention
grabbing your attention

Look. There is a thing
over there.
You point grasping at the space
in between you and everything.
Let's go!

I run with the cart,
kick my legs
and jump on the back.

Let's go!

The Garden on the Hillside

We have a garden on the
hillside.

Over the years
it's been both
sparse and
lush
full of flowers
and
other
small vegetables
depending on the sun.

Each year
we trim away the weeds
brush the top layer
of dried dirt
and leaves
and make a new plan.

Different variations on a theme.
Some years tomatoes
and jalapenos

Others just more basil

I tried pumpkins a few times
but the beasties eat them first

I never gave up though
maybe this will be the year
of the pumpkin

A large one, we can carve

We caged the veggies in last year.
Carpentry and chicken wire
saving each struggling sprout.

So far,
the greenery is gently trellising
for peas
and
leaves of lettuce
flop forwards ready to eat.

Above the garden terrace
Blackberries which we
mistook for raspberries
lay their traps.

Their spikes and pointy thorns
are gnarled and

stick like barbed wire

While the jasmine
our very same jasmine
smoothly and deftly
stretches its limbs

You're likely to trip over
a loose brick or grapevine

so
tread gently
and handle with careful attention

for the best blueberry
Is the one you pick yourself
before the birds get to it.

Learning to Draw

Learning to draw was hard
it took me
years

Each time I'd try
it would look
so
very
wrong

And my heart would hurt
and I'd
scrunch up the paper
until it was unrecognizable

and wait until I'd forgotten
how bad I thought I was
to try
again

the next time
felt even worse
I could never erase enough
to make the wrong lines

disappear

crumple. crumple.

Why. Was. It. So. Hard?

Why was everyone better?

crumple. crumple.

The hardest part, choosing what
to
draw

start simple
a line
then a circle
a shape that looks like a triangle
but round

connect it
to the
next part
to make the next
part

part, part, whole
until you can start to tell what
it is supposed to be.

That's how I learned to draw
a piece at a time.

Want the whole thing?
Take a picture.
Want to see the sum
of the parts?
Draw.

There is still erasing.
Lots of erasing.
But we are on better terms,
my eraser and I.

I love that I can always
remove, undo.

That I can always
try again.

Go Read a Book

Go read a book
or seven
or a hundred.

Hoard them around you
like a dragon's stash.
Each a treasure waiting to be devoured.

Hunker down
Underneath the softest blanket
Shutting out everything but
Chapter 1

Ignore
the dedication,
you already know it was written for you
and others like
you
who know that the secret
to travel lies not in a boat
or a train
but by book

You have permission
to skim the forward

best not let someone tell you their thoughts
before you've tasted the story
yourself.

Skip the table of contents
I find chapter titles
give much too much
away

Take one last breath
then,
dive deeply into
the moment of the first
sentence.

Once your under
begin to explore,
get your bearings

and as your eyes and
mind
adjust to the changing
light

Put
your trust in the voice
the one you hear in your head as
you read

let it hypnotize you
and lull you
into being
a willing participant
in the narrative

As the world dissolves around you
begin Chapter 2.

Pizza

We make pizza
here

We make pizza
a lot

More than the national
average

Almost as much
as we brush our teeth

Pizza
the cure for the Sunday blues

Monday is coming
but its
better
because, there will be pizza
for lunch.

What will you put on your pizza?
The same toppings every week?
Tried and true?

Or adventure ridden,
with new pizza permutations
to try?

Mushroom, spinach and cheese?
Artichoke, jalapeno, pineapple?
Salami, mozzarella, arugula?

We don't judge people,
by their pizza toppings.

We will love you
no matter what
you put
on your
pizza.

Here and How

Here and now
there is a choice
of here and how.

Here are my hands,
How can I help?
or
How can you help me?

Here is my understanding,
How can I strengthen it?
or
How can I ignore the pieces that
don't fit?

Here is my best,
How can I improve?
or
How can I get by?

Here is my
voice,
How can I use it to speak up
for voiceless others?
or

How can I avoid
confrontation?

Here is my choice,
How can I
choose best?
or
How to best choose?

I trust you.

The Right Track

You might notice
something
strange

A penny on the ground
when you were just
thinking
about
presidents

Your favorite meal
at home
when you were
wishing it was
for dinner

The person in
your math problem
has your name
and a sister
with the same name
as your cousin
or aunt

You and your

best friend
wear the very same
outfit
and you didn't
even plan it.

I call these
the sign posts.
They tell you
You are on
the right
trail.

Lift your eyes
off the ground
and look for more.

Then, keep
living the way you have been
because
you are on the
right
track.

The Pineapple

You may have heard
that there is
a
legend
in our family.

The infamous
pineapple.

It is a story of giggles
and sneaking.
Laughing until you
can't breath
and
then laughing some more

I'll tell you about it
one day,
but here's all you really
need to know...

In our family,
A pineapple means
someone is thinking of you.

A pineapple means
we make each other smile

A pineapple means
its okay if things get a little
squishy

A pineapple means
we help when we can

Like the ancient
Hawaiians,
a pineapple means
we
are each other's
home

Precious Pieces

There will be a day,
when you are too angry to speak
to me.

I will have done something
to rock the floor of your world
instead of your cradle.

You'll stomp, scream, and
maybe cry.

When that's all out,
over and done
and you get real quiet
in your room.

And you think,
What's next?
How do I go back out there,
where she is?

In that stillness,
imagine a slivered section
of my heart.
Divided up into pieces

of things I will
never
stop
loving.

For even when I
am angry,
I will always
hang on to the precious piece
that says
I love you.

The Koi Pond

Fish slither under the darkened surface
They stalk the buzzing flies
Leaping from the waters
Hunger in their eyes

The minnows, what are left of them
Follow in their wake
Trailing like a puppy dog
The koi can never shake

Water flows down the crevices
As falls the waterfall,
While elephant ears sway gently
Under the willow's leafy shawl

This is a very special place
It's right outside your window
The rushing water plays a song,
The bubbling pond's crescendo.

Bedtime

Bedtime
it's the very best
time of night

You're afraid you might
miss out on what's happening

Bedtime.

You're afraid of the dark
and your body is shivering

Bedtime.

You're afraid you won't fall
asleep.
Your focus unwavering.

But trust me little one
Bedtime
is the very best
time.

The time to sleep so your body can grow
The time to dream by the pond light's glow

The time for the stars to light the skies
The time to rest and to close your eyes

Goodnight little one
I promise I will wake you soon
After the dance
of the phase of the moon

I Don't Know What I'm Doing

I don't know what I'm doing
I feel this way a lot
I don't know what I'm doing
More often-er than not

I don't know what I'm doing
Though I'm always ready on the spot
I don't know what I'm doing
But look prepared in every shot

I don't know what I'm doing
I'm often quite distraught
I don't know what I'm doing
and it's time that someone taught

We don't know what we're doing
Nobody really does
We don't know what we're doing
and it's all the same because

Till we do know what we're doing
We must have patience by the score
Until we all know what we're doing
and don't have to pretend anymore.

www.ingramcontent.com/pod-product-compliance
Lightning Source LLC
Chambersburg PA
CBHW051744130826
49812CB00033B/993